CORPORATIONS SUCK:
BEAT THEM AT THEIR OWN GAME

by Lucas Anderssen

Copyright © Lucas Anderssen 2018. All rights reserved.

No part of this publication may be reproduced, stored in a retrieval system, or transmitted in any form or by any means without the prior written permission of the author and publisher.

This book is for informational and entertainment purposes only and is not intended to provide financial or legal advice. The author and publisher specifically disclaim any liability, loss or risk, personal or otherwise, that is incurred directly or indirectly as a result of the use of any of the information described in this book.

I learned the importance of using these words while working in Corporate America.

First Edition

First Published in 2018

KDP ISBN: 9781726837835

About the Author

I'm a middle-aged man living in Middle America. I will go out of my way to help people, even total strangers. Several times in my life I have found keys or phones or wallets loaded with cash and I've gone out of my way to get everything back to the rightful owner. I have done volunteer work for many years and have donated thousands of hours of my life and considerable amounts of money to them. I donate to charities regularly and tip generously. I have developed a life-long policy of never stealing from people, volunteer organizations or small businesses. I don't shoplift, I don't do carding and I don't steal identities. However, when it comes to dealing with corporations, I think everyone has the right to be opportunistic.

I have worked in multiple positions as an employee and as a manager in Corporate America for over twenty five years. I consistently see how corporations operate in a way that's detrimental to their employees. However there are many opportunities to beat the corporations at their own game. This book highlights many of the issues with corporations from the employee's perspective. But more importantly, it tells you how you can do something about it, instead of living a life of quiet suffering.

Anderssen is also the author of the unique, powerful book: How To Scam Corporations.

TABLE OF CONTENTS

Introduction 5

Corporations Suck 6

Do Not Drink The Kool-Aid 9

Your Employer is Stealing From You 11

Enough is Enough 14

Change Your Mindset 15

Have a Friend at Work 17

Run A Side Business 18

Be Aware of Corporate Surveillance 19

Social Engineering 20

Maximizing Your Income 22

Helping Others 23

Helping Yourself 24

Maximizing Benefits 29

Embezzling Expenses 31

Making Free Phone Calls 34

Death Benefits 36

Kickbacks and Payoffs 38

Stealing Time 40

Faking Disability 43

Intellectual Property 46

Suing Your Employer 47
Do Not Break The Company 49
Think Long Term 50
Becoming a Whistleblower 53
Exiting a Company 55
Summary 57

Introduction

Corporations suck. There, I said it. But didn't you already know that? Every day millions of employees trudge into work hating something about their working existence. Maybe they hate their boss. It could be some of their co-workers. Or it might be the nature of the work itself they are required to do. Every day all these disgruntled employees try to come up with a way to escape. Here are a few ideas they've had:

I'm going to retire early.
I'm going to quit and work for the competition.
I'm going on disability.
I'm going to quit and start my own business.
I'm going to shoot up this place and everyone in it.

Does this sound familiar? Ever had any of these thoughts? There's one big reason you haven't done any one of these things: money. You need that job to support your lifestyle and your habits. Your employer pays for your medical insurance. Maybe you have college debt, a mortgage or a family to support. Starting your own business can be extremely challenging and time-consuming. Retiring or going on disability will result in a big pay cut. Shooting up the place is not recommended and will have the obvious consequences. Going to work for the competition won't change anything: you'll end up with the same lifestyle, and you'll just be working with people who have different names.

There have been many books written on how to get out of sucky corporate life by starting up on your own. This is not one of them. You can quit if you hate it, but if you want to stay, there are some creative things you can do which will enhance your life there. Some of them are ethical, some are not. That's what this book is about.

Corporations Suck

Corporations have become a necessary evil. We all enjoy the products of the corporations: the vehicles, the food, the entertainment. But, to be more specific it is working life in the corporations that really sucks. It is all the things that we as corporate minions have to endure every day just to get a paycheck and to continue to have health insurance benefits. Wherever you work you will be experiencing some stress and discomfort for at least one of these reasons: untrustworthy senior management, an unreasonable boss, evil co-workers, job tasks that you hate, feeling neglected when you are no longer invited to meetings, being assigned a new role, not being assigned a new role, lack of empowerment, long working hours, low pay, poor benefits, unsafe working conditions, future uncertainty. The list goes on.

There are so many ways in which working for corporations sucks. Companies have a mantra that consists of a mission statement and some guiding principles that get rammed down employees' throats. Most of us have minimal respect for our managers. One of mine likes to compare us to her young children and how she raises them. She obviously has an unhappy home life and this reflects on the way we are all treated. So often I have seen people with the wrong talent become managers. Many don't seem to understand that it takes a unique set of skills to lead others. Managers frequently lack training, which is a large factor in the pain that employees feel. Because of their inability to lead, managers often have no patience with employees, resulting in employees being fired when they just needed some additional assistance. Many employees are not being given a fair chance to show what they can do and if they run into personal issues managers are often not there to help. Where I work we had a young man who was very good at what he did and had been doing good work for about two years. Unfortunately he had health problems and took time off at random times. He was mentally ill and became suicidal. Rather than helping him, his manager fired him.

Management likes to refer to us as "family" which is so ironic. Would you treat your family members the way you are treated by the corporation?

The bigger they are the more bureaucratic they become, worrying about optimizing details that you have to tend to. Bigger companies usually have more issues than smaller, leaner types. Publicly-traded corporations tend to be the worst. Many companies have no soul. They all started small, usually founded by someone with a desire to change the world and to make a difference. Then they grew either organically or by acquisition. At some point the founder with all the passion to hold things together left and his successors had a different focus, usually their own.

You have to accept the fact that there will always be people in life that you have issues with. All of us have at least one co-worker that we don't get along with. Many are either negative, chronic complainers, gossipers, or they are overbearing, boorish or offensive in some other way. When we chose our friends we have options. Our co-workers are chosen for us.

If you are in a position where you have to bill your time to clients, you are no doubt feeling the pressure to bill more hours to bring in more profits. This often means billing more for less work carried out. But it could also mean working late into the night for The Man.

If you feel like you are entitled to more money, you have to figure out a game that consists of sucking up to the boss and competing with your coworkers. Opportunities for promotions do exist but the process we have to go through to get one is usually frustrating. We're told there's no budget for it this year, or that our performance wasn't quite perfect enough. Or we see our co-workers get promoted quicker than us, when we feel we're more worthy. If we are able to get promoted it's probably because we sold our souls to the company and became one of the people we despised not so long ago. To get ahead we will have spent less time with our families and our children will spend more time doing unhealthy activities, playing video games, surfing the internet and having no role model. To get ahead in corporate life your best bet is often to go somewhere else. But where?

In order to be profitable, most companies have figured out it's more cost-effective to hire people through temporary agencies. This eliminates the need to pay employees benefits, allows them to pay a much lower salary and to see if that employee might be worthy of becoming a permanent employee sometime in the future. There are several problems with this approach. The employer has to pay a 30 – 50% up-charge to the agency for every hour the temp works. The temp suffers as he doesn't get any benefits.

Also, it creates a class system at the place of employment, with the temp being the lowest class. This class system is detrimental to a positive work environment and the temps tend to be even more disgruntled than regular employees. It is much easier for employers to hire temps over regular employees in this way, say for special projects, as they don't have to have senior management justify a full time employee (or "head count"). However, what tends to happen is the temp stays a long time and the class system is perpetuated, as there really is no definition of "temporary". In most states it's up to the employer to decide what's best.

Essentially, in Corporate America we all feel like slaves or small cogs in a big wheel: insignificant and inconsequential. Attempts to make changes either to the corporation or for our own benefit often hit a wall. We see executives, people no better than us, making outlandish salaries and bonuses. If we are managers we can't manage the way we want to because of stiff corporate cultures, upper management ineptness or budgetary constraints. We sit through tedious meetings and feel endless emotional pain. If we aren't careful our morale suffers, we become more and more negative and jaded. And we do all it so that we can get a paycheck.

Do Not Drink The Kool-Aid

Senior management has to report to the board of directors or the owners about how they are making the company more profitable. In most cases they don't really know how to do this and they don't know how the company actually operates. In order to grow profits, they lean on management below them to each grow their piece of the business. As a result, all kinds of wild statements get made to employees to get them to perform.

Let's say the company has just been put up for sale. Executives know that the moment most employees hear about this they will become nervous about losing their jobs, so will start job hunting. So, executives are very careful about when they announce the sale of the company and how they word it. They are always very quick to point out how wonderful the sale of the company will be and how all employees will be better off under the new owners. They try to have employees believe their jobs are safe. They go out of their way to sound excited and say whatever they feel they have to so as to motivate employees into working hard and not quitting. Sounding excited is usually pretty easy for executives in this situation, as they know that they will be getting a large payout when the trade takes place. If you are a young, naïve employee, you might believe all this positive talk and merrily trudge ahead, assuming that your job will be safe. Executives don't have much choice but to encourage people to stay. The reality is that in most cases they don't really know what the future will hold for regular employees. It's possible they do know about major layoff plans, but they can't announce them. If they did, employees would quit in droves, things would fall apart and the value of the company would plummet. Whenever there's uncertainty in an organization, it's the most employable people who leave first. Those whose performance is below par or those who interview poorly, or who lack self-confidence tend to stay as they have difficulty finding alternative employment. Senior management knows they need to keep the best people. Always keep your options open whenever there is any job uncertainty. Remember, you must have your best interests at heart. Make sure that you are well networked in life and aware of other opportunities that exist and apply for them. Always have a goal of moving forward and progressing in your life and career. You do not want to be moving backwards if you chose to make a job change.

I have found it's always best to put myself in the shoes of other people. What would I do if I were in senior management's situation? Why are they doing what they are doing? Don't believe what the executives tell you. Just as you have your best interests at heart, so do they. Their only goal is making themselves look as good as they can to maximize their income. Is that your goal?

Your Employer is Stealing From You

It may be very subtle, but your employer is stealing from you. Corporations are in business to make money. You are there to make others wealthy. Each company is made up of smaller groups/divisions managed by someone. That manager is financially responsible for her little piece of the company & if there is any way she can find to improve profitability of her group, she'll get a nice pat on the head and a bigger bonus. Because she's regularly having meetings with her superiors who are beating on her to improve profitability of her fiefdom, if she sees a way to do that she will. That includes selling products and services for more money. It also includes having staff do more with less. There are many ways to do more with less including not paying employees the going rate for the job, denying promotions and vacations or not paying staff equally. It's usually in the company's interest to have employees be exempt (from overtime) so they can be forced to work for long hours at no additional pay.

What employers also like to do is to not replace people when they leave. Let's say there's a group of five people in a department, doing essentially the same function. If one of them retires or quits, it's not automatic that the department's supervisor will be allowed to replace that person. Word gets out to senior management that the person is gone and the supervisor has to justify the need for the replacement. In some cases senior management allows the headcount replacement, but in another department. When someone leaves there's usually a vacancy there for several weeks or months, sometimes indefinitely. The end result is that the remaining staff have to pick up the slack left by the departing employee. They feel the pressure of all the additional work and have to work longer hours, skipping breaks, foregoing vacations so the work gets done. If the supervisor sees the work is being done, the decision is made not to replace the person who left. Soon they forget they used to have an additional employee and the pressure on the remaining employees to perform becomes the new norm. Every now and again the supervisor will bring donuts into work to thank employees for their dedication. The days of employees working 9 – 5 are long gone. Don't forget that they will lay you off in a heartbeat if the budget changes.

Managers have to operate within a budget which is set at the beginning of each fiscal year & monitored regularly. They look bad if they blow their budget and get recognized in lavish ways if their group does well financially. It's very much in their interest to keep expenses low, and since the company's biggest expense is employees' salaries this is the area that gets the biggest attention. Sometimes an employee is hourly paid and needs to work a lot of hours on a project. Managers would then decide to make that employee exempt so that person can be paid less. Women and minorities are deliberately paid less than white males, since raising their salaries to equalize things would cost the company big time. Employers deliberately keep salaries a secret and encourage employees not to discuss salary, since if word got out about the inequality there would be problems.

Managers like to give their employees laptops and cell phones to keep them on a leash and have them feel obligated to work longer hours. An employee with a laptop or company cell phone is likely to take it on vacation with them to do the corporation's work 24/7.

Wage theft, that is, theft of employees' wages by corporations, is at an all time high. Wage theft can take several forms, but mostly it consists of employers just not paying employees what they should be receiving. According to one study, the US dollar amounts of wage theft greatly exceed that of other crimes, like burglary and auto theft. Some store employees are required to keep working after they've clocked out. Immigrant workers are often not paid the full amount for the work they have done, as employers know they can get away with it. Temporary or seasonal workers also get abused in this way: they are promised a certain wage, then when they've done the work they get paid less. The sad fact is that there are many employers out there who simply do not treat employees with respect or dignity. Many companies are run by individuals who are out for their own gain, often at the expense of the employee.

Your employer is also stealing your health, raising your blood pressure, causing you to forego your well being in favor of company profits. If you're not careful, corporate stress can drive you to overeat, gain weight and under-exercise. You run the risk of smoking, drinking and gambling more.

The most significant thing your employer is taking from you is your time. As a corporate slave you will never get that time back. As they say: money comes and goes, but only time goes. Is working at that company what you really want to be doing with your time? If not, figure out a way to get out. If you've decided to stay, read on.

ENOUGH IS ENOUGH

That's enough complaining and negativity. I'm beginning to feel like I've spent the day at work with some of my negative co-workers. So, you've decided that you don't want to quit your employer right now but you have to make some changes. The good news is that there is a lot you can do in your current environment. You have to decide which of these approaches you want to take in order to fight back against the corporations that don't have your best interests at heart.

It's time for action.

Change Your Mindset

The first thing to do is to accept the situation you're in and decide to make a change. Understand that the corporation is an entity unto itself that is determined to make money. Starting today, your personal interests are much more important than theirs. You need to accept the fact that working in Corporate America (or any other country) will not give you a fulfilling lifestyle. Be aware that all the issues you are experiencing are external forces and what you are feeling is your personal response to these. You should also know that you are not alone and that the vast majority of people working in corporate life feel what you are feeling.

It is critically important to have interests outside of your work. If you are totally consumed by life at the corporation you will become a very boring person: boring to others and boring to yourself. When the axe falls (and fall it will) and you are a victim of downsizing or synergy, you need to have talents and interests to fall back on. There are many external interests you could develop, such as sports, side businesses, hobbies or working out. Side interests will also help you to avoid being sucked down by the corporation. Find your passion & pursue it.

Have a positive outlook on life. Refuse to be put down by the corporate types. Make a conscious decision not to associate with negative people; only hang out with those who have a positive outlook. This is true with all people you interact with, but is especially true for your co-workers, as you'll be spending forty hours or more with them every week. If they have a negative effect on you, the less time you spend with them the better.

One of the reasons that most employees feel like trapped slaves is that they think like consumers. They assume that working for The Man is all they are capable of. Breaking out of that thinking is critical to breaking away from corporate slavery. Think like a producer, someone who is making and selling things into society, rather than as just a consumer or a doer of other people's tasks. Always think about what's important to you in life, whether it's family, friends, good health and being a good, decent person to other people. Obviously, money is necessary for survival in this society, but be aware of the importance of its balance with lifestyle.

Visualize someone you see as a positive influence on people and whom you admire. Observe what they do and how they do it. Stand tall, be proud and refuse to be pushed around. Rise above the herd. Do your best to become an employee who could get a job anywhere because they are confident in their abilities. Dress well, be calm, clear and sophisticated. Eat healthy food and drink plenty of water. Exercise; it's a tremendous destressor. Keep your chin up and keep putting one foot in front of the other. Life is too short to be living someone else's dream.

Remember that only you have your best interests at heart. Your manager, co-workers, senior management, the human resources department are only focused on themselves, so that is where your focus should be.

Have a Friend at Work

Some years back I attended a one day seminar called "How to Work With Difficult People". I was all excited when I signed up for this course. I was fairly new to the corporate world and finally I was going to find out how to handle those co-workers of mine that I had the most trouble dealing with. The first topic the trainer covered with us was an extensive questionnaire about ourselves. There was question after question, mostly relating to the types of environments we prefer, how we handle situations and our personalities. After answering all the questions we analyzed our own data and it placed us in one of four quadrants. The trainer then explained that depending on the quadrant you were in, you would have the most difficulty dealing with people in one of the other quadrants. He was right! The people we have the most issues with depend on our own personality attributes. Just because you have issues with a particular person, doesn't mean that others will find them problematic.

Instead of being antagonistic towards your co-workers, it's a good idea to have some friends at work with whom you can share discussions. These discussions should not take the form of complaining, but should focus on what each of you is going to do different to make positive changes for each other and maybe others. Avoid negative co-workers when you decide who you're going to associate with.

Some of these relationships could blossom into affairs and that's perfectly fine. Romantic encounters keep life interesting. Even if the relationship ends it's usually possibly for the two of you to work together. Avoid sleeping with your boss or a subordinate: as the saying goes, you don't want to shit on your own doorstep. Rest assured that it is amazingly difficult to keep affairs from becoming public knowledge. You may think you are trying really hard to separate your work and love lives but even a glance at each other will be picked up by perceptive co-workers.

Run A Side Business

This is not a book about setting up and running a company. But why not consider operating a side business or hobby and doing it while you're at work. People with creativity make crafts at home to sell online. People with mechanical skills make their own furniture or repair vehicles in their spare time. Others with accounting skills help people with their income taxes returns every year. Some aspects of running a business needs to be done during the day: selling the items online, setting up new jobs, handling payments, for example. Do these things while you are at work. Look at your work schedule and how you interact with others. Identify times and locations where you won't be disturbed so you can handle things. Maybe there's a conference room that nobody uses at certain times of the day. Do you notice that most of your co-workers are gone every Tuesday? You should be able to find some time to do things like this that are important to you. If you're not sure, look around and get creative.

If you chose to run a side business while you work at a corporation, I recommend keeping that as quiet as you can. It's possible that others will be fine with it and it's possible they won't. If for some reason in the future your corporate work is not up to par, your boss could use your side business as an excuse and encourage you to shut it down. Some companies require you to sign a pre-employment agreement, including a stipulation that you won't have any other paid employment while you work there. This is totally unreasonable and another thing that sucks about corporate life. Here's another reason not to divulge your private work life to managers and co-workers: it's none of their business.

BE AWARE OF CORPORATE SURVEILLANCE

Don't underestimate your manager's perceptive talents. He became a manager for a reason and has probably been in your situation himself. He is watching your behavior and if he senses that you are not putting in a full days' work, there could be consequences. You operate on a knife-edge in some respects and a fine line exists between being seen to be doing the job you are paid for and putting yourself first. Only you can figure this out. Be aware too that the company knows when you access non-work related websites using their equipment/network. Managers can easily have the IT department run a report indicating what your computer has been up to.

It's always in your best interests to have your manager actually like you. One of the best ways to get eliminated from a managers department is to have your boss dislike you for some reason. Just as there are co-workers that you have difficulty with it's possible that your manager has issues with you, simply due to a clash of personalities. Being aware of this is critical. If you become aware of it you can try to avoid spending too much time with him, try to address the personality issue he has problems with or attempt to move to another department or company.

Social Engineering

Social engineering is the art of persuading others to do something they would not normally do. It's a relatively new term that encompasses a wide variety of confidence tricks, where the objective is to gather information, gain access to systems or facilities, or just get money or goods. At some time or another you will need to develop good social engineering skills. It helps if you have good people skills, are naturally persuasive and have the ability to lie and be convincing, as this is at the heart of good social engineering. We all do this to some extent. Think about the times when you were young and needed your parents to take you somewhere. Or when you tried to get your first job and had to convince the hiring manager you could handle it. Or when you wanted to go on a date with someone. Every day we face situations where we need to be able to convince someone to do something.

Start by visualizing yourself getting whatever it is you want. Imagine how you are going to achieve this and whom you need to convince. Realize that whomever you need to persuade has wants, needs and desires too and they will not take kindly to being verbally abused. They are more likely to help you to get what you want if you are viewed as a considerate person who has a need. Remember that people do business with and are willing to work with other people who they know, like and trust. The person you are working on needs to know you and a few things about you. It often helps to establish a common bond between you and the person you are trying to socially engineer, whether it's the state you both lived in, where you have both vacationed, people you both know or some other common interest you can ferret out. If you have the opportunity to do some research on the person you need to get help from, this will speed up the social engineering process.

When trying to convince others to do something, it's important to be calm, polite but persistent. Sometimes you'll get objections, so just politely restate your request or position. Once you've firmly but politely made your statement three times in a row the other person will often see your determination and either give you what you want, or won't.

If you try to conduct social engineering by phone, one challenge can be just getting the person you are calling to answer and speak to you. One useful utility here is FIRErtc, which allows you to spoof your actual caller ID. Download the free app, decide which company you want to pretend to belong to and use your PC or smart phone to make calls.

Entire books have been written on the subject of social engineering and the purpose of this section is not to reproduce other works, but to make you aware that it's something you need to be good at if you are to succeed in life. Only people who want to live dull lives on the straight and narrow don't need these skills. I believe there's a very thin line between what is right and wrong, legal and illegal, ethical and immoral. It's much more exciting to live life close to that line.

Maximizing Your Income

Every department in every company has a budget for expenses. Your goal should be to get as much of these as you are entitled too, and more. Think about expenses that your employer has. These will include travel for trips to suppliers, customers or trade shows. Companies pay for cell phones, laptops, company cars, meals while traveling and many other things. Position yourself in the company so that you can get some of these legitimately. Ask for them. Convince your manager that you are doing a good job and can do even more to maximize company profits if only you had (fill in the blanks here). In later sections I'll show you how to get money from your employer in less legitimate ways. But first you have to figure out the right way to do it.

Let's say you are a low level employee in the accounting department. You have seen that your manager has allowed your coworkers to go to conferences occasionally. You've never been to a conference before, but identify one that you think might be beneficial. Observe how your manager operates and make sure you chose a good opportunity to approach her about going to this. Catch her when she's in a good mood, after she's received some good news or at some other time that seems best. Use your best social engineering skills to convince her as to why you attending will be so good for the department and the company. Get her perspective on conferences and trade shows and listen attentively to her responses. Offer to do some of the things she suggests would be beneficial while you are there. Make sure you understand the company's policies on travel, how to book flights, hotel rooms and rental cars. Be aware that there are good and bad times of the year to be spending company money. Towards the end of the fiscal year, companies often clamp down on excessive expenditures, as they want the end of year financial statements to look as rosy as possible for the investors. This might not be a good time to ask to attend an event you've never been to before. Instead, do your research early in the fiscal year and get your boss's approval sooner rather than later.

Helping Others

Here in the USA we live in an every-man-for-himself society. There is a safety net to help people who run into problems, financial or otherwise, but it has big holes in it. In some other countries the safety net is more intact to help people. Executives and senior managers are not so heavily rewarded as they are in the USA, relative to typical working people. You can argue the pros and cons of these different societies, but the reality is that we need to help each other much more in the USA, as governments are not so inclined to do so. As a result, I am advocating that when you are an employee for a company and you see someone embezzling, turn a blind eye. I have done this on numerous occasions. As a manager I wouldn't go out of my way to tell an employee to steal from the company, but if I saw something shady taking place I would deliberately let it happen, unless there was any risk of someone being hurt. I had employees who needed some company product, so I let them take it. I've mentored fellow employees who wanted to start up their own business in direct conflict with our current employer. I've been aware of other coworkers who've taken items they needed and I don't rat out my fellow employee. I do this because it's the right thing to do. An added benefit is that they are less likely to rat me out.

What this means is that if you work in the finance department of a company and you suspect some employee fraud is happening, let it slide. Do you work in a hospital and see someone trying to cheat the system? Ignore it. Maybe you're a manager and you see an employee taking too much time off: let it happen. We all need to work together to help each other in subtle ways to beat the system. We can't allow total anarchy to take over. The companies we work for still need to function. However, helping each other out helps to level out the severely tilted playing field. If everyone was more like this I am convinced that capitalistic societies would be better places.

HELPING YOURSELF

In addition to helping others, it's time to help yourself, as a high percentage of corporate employees have been doing for decades. What I am referring to here is stealing from your employer. This is something that you are either OK doing or you are not. Before you reject this idea outright, ask yourself if you have ever taken anything from them that didn't belong to you. Maybe you took a pen home accidentally. What did you do when you realized that you had it? Did you return it immediately? Or did you continue to use it? How guilty did you feel with the knowledge that you had stolen from your employer? Did you rationalize this by thinking about the injustices that exist between employees and corporations? Did you reflect on any co-workers who had been treated unfairly at work? Do you feel, as I do, that it is totally wrong to steal from individuals, charities, not-for-profit organizations and small businesses? Do you feel it is acceptable to be opportunistic with corporations, as they are in the way they treat employees and other companies?

Stealing from your employer is something that you either find acceptable or you don't. If you do not, be aware that much of the rest of this book focuses on how this can be accomplished. Whichever your position on this subject, I totally respect your choice.

As you read through the future sections, there will be some approaches that you find acceptable and some that you do not. Everyone draws the line in different places. Even if you disagree with the concept of theft from corporations, I do suggest you read to the end of the book, so that you are aware of different ways that others are taking to supplement their incomes and to get a small amount of revenge on the company. Some day this information may be useful to you. What follows is a collection of theft angles I have personally seen in over 25 years of life in Corporate America.

Look around you at work. What do you see? What kind of security exists in the building where you work? In many cases you will find it easy to take home small items that are used around your work place on a daily basis. Slipping smaller items in pockets is more explainable if you are confronted than having items in a purse or bag. When walking out with items or taking anything that doesn't belong to you, be aware of how guilty you might look. Act confidently. Don't look shifty. Don't look around in a furtive way. Have an image in your mind that what you are taking is for legitimate purposes. Be prepared with a plausible explanation if confronted about what you are doing. Think about how you walk, act, talk & appear when you are not stealing company items and practice this when you're lifting from your employer too. As you walk out, visualize yourself doing what you enjoy the most, whether it's fishing, shopping or having sex. Your body language is critical to what others think of you. It's been said that when someone speaks they may or may not be telling the truth. But their body language does not lie.

If there's a first aid kit in your workplace, you shouldn't need to buy Band-Aids or antiseptic wipes at the store. Pens, tape and paperclips fit in your pockets easily. Notepads often look alike whether you bought them from a store or stole them from your employer. Does your cell phone need charging? Use your employer's electricity. Is free coffee available at work? Don't stop at Starbucks on your way in. Need batteries at home for electronics? You will probably find that your employer has some.

I don't advocate shoplifting, but a common trick used by established shoplifters is to wear baggy clothing to conceal items. Some creative shoplifters have fabricated some elaborate pants and skirts to cleverly hide large boxes. If you plan to use it, research this technique to make sure that what you wear doesn't give your game away. To be less conspicuous, wear baggy clothing regularly, even when you are not taking home items from your employer.

One of the best ways to avoid being caught is to take items that don't get counted or tracked in any way. Management doesn't care if you take a paperclip home from the office because nobody is counting them. Someone buys a big box, puts it in a cabinet and anyone can take what they need. When the box is empty somebody will buy another one. On the other hand, the company's finances are being tracked by a team of people and if money isn't where it should be, questions get asked. If it's a significant amount of money there will be an investigation. This is also true of expensive property owned by a company, referred to as capital assets. These are things with a large dollar value, such as photocopiers, company vehicles and production equipment. Capital items like these often have a tag or sticker on them with an asset code number. Think about the kinds of things you encounter that are not being tracked: towels and toiletries in hotel rooms;

bowls, silverware, napkins and straws in restaurants; stationary items in an office; shop towels at a car repair shop. Once you have these at home it's unlikely anyone will come looking for them.

If you take something large that you know will be missed, think about the investigation that will take place. If you were the investigator what would you do? Who would you question and what approaches would you take? Suppose for a moment you embezzled some funds from the corporate coffers. What kind of paper trail did you leave behind you? Many paper trails are electronic in nature, so does this point to a computer that you use? Can you thwart this by using another computer? Are you taking money on your last day working for that company? If so how will they try to reach you? Did you lift a piece of equipment you plan to sell on eBay? Does it have a serial number? Did a security camera capture you? Anticipate every question and every rabbit hole that investigators will go down. In many cases you only (!) have to survive six years, the statute of limitations in most US states for any kind of civil action to be taken against you.

I often need to photocopy items at work for a volunteer organization I'm involved with. I have figured out the routines of my coworkers and boss and make sure I do this at a time and in a way that will avoid any confrontation from anyone. I stand at the copier with a folder containing work-related papers while I copy. As copies are spat out I carefully place them in my folder.

Don't discuss stealing company property with anyone. Trust nobody. You may think that someone there is your friend and that you can trust them, but you will sleep much better at night knowing that only you have the dirt on what you are doing. Many companies, especially those who have been crime victims before, will set up anonymous tip lines where people can rat on their fellow employees. Sometimes, to mitigate theft, managers will deliberately rotate employees from one role to another. This is partly to see if a theft problem disappears and partly as a matter of course to keep employees off balance and to keep them from being complacent. Other companies establish random audits, even if they have not seen theft issues. The point here is to be wary of managers and fellow employees at all times and not to divulge what you're up to.

Some employers try to minimize theft by instituting a code of ethics, which involves watching videos, regular training and re-training on topics relating to ethical behavior. They can tout this positively with customers and stockholders and it makes managers feel good and have something positive to talk about. This can be a good thing if you have your act together and know how to commit crimes. Managers feel more comfortable when they think you have gone through this training so might be less likely to suspect you of theft. Make sure you take the training and don't complain about it. Some companies want employees to take employee satisfaction surveys. These are carried out to gage how employees feel about all kinds of topics. Having been the survey taker on numerous occasions and been a manager reviewing the results I can say with confidence that these surveys are a total waste of time and money. Most managers feel obliged to deal with negative survey feedback and don't really care about having to make any changes to address problems that they reveal. I have never seen any changes come about as a result of employee opinion surveys. Most employees don't take them seriously, for good reason. However, if a high percentage of employees give very negative feedback on ethics issues this can raise a red flag that something needs to be investigated. You don't want this to happen. I usually fill out these surveys over a cup of coffee and do my best to give answers I think managers want to hear.

What happens if you are confronted about stealing? Be paranoid and expect it to happen at some point if you take items from your employer. Always be prepared to have a response for any situation so you don't appear flustered. Having some degree of plausible deniability is very important. If I was approached about my photocopying I'd openly admit that yes, I'm making these copies and thought the company was all in favor of helping volunteer organizations; I know other people do it. If I was asked why I was walking out with a box of papers at the end of the day I might smile and state that I'm going to a meeting the next day. Your exact situation will vary depending on the company, your position and other factors.

Some years ago a long-time employee was spotted pushing a wheelbarrow out of a facility. The security guard stopped him and asked him what was in the wheelbarrow. "Nothing", said the man. Not trusting him, the security guard closely inspected the wheelbarrow. Finding nothing suspicious he let the man go. Next day the same thing happened; yet again the guard could find nothing hidden in the wheelbarrow. When it happened for a third time, the security guard had the tire removed to see what was hidden inside: nothing. This went on for some time, then the man quit. Some time later the security guard spotted the man in a store and confronted him: "I know you were up to something; what were you stealing?" "Wheelbarrows" said the man.

Pilfering in plain sight can be done and this story illustrates that.

You might find that, despite all of your best efforts you get pulled into an unexpected meeting and confronted with some awkward facts or allegations about items you've stolen. Whenever you have to attend a meeting with your boss and human resources people, you should always be on your guard. Handle the meeting calmly and confidently without getting angry or upset. Don't cry or make any outbursts. Maintain your composure. If you are confronted with unavoidable facts, you don't want to insult the intelligence of others. But this is where you hope that your value to the company exceeds their desire to terminate you for theft. If you are fired, do your best to defend yourself. Ask yourself if you are able to take legal action against them, possibly due to discrimination or harassment. If so, bringing up this fact at the confrontation meeting might help minimize the risk of you being terminated for theft. This topic is covered in more detail later.

Where you are in the corporation affects what you can take. You might think that climbing the corporate ladder and becoming an executive will afford greater riches from scamming, but I have not seen this to be the case. Often it's the people towards the middle or below with some level of authority they can abuse can make out the best. The higher up you are in the corporate world, the more visible you are to subordinates. Most employees develop some kind of inner glow when they see the boss screw up as it reminds them that they too are human and fallible. So when employees see the boss embezzling, disgruntled employees tend to discuss it and report it.

MAXIMIZING BENEFITS

Many companies offer health insurance, dental care and other benefits to their employees, partly out of tradition, partly to keep their employees as healthy as necessary to do their work and partly because competitive companies are doing it. If you have a job that offers benefits, you are usually able to get insurance coverage for your spouse and children. When you are first hired you go through a process to register them and have them set up in your employer's database. This is where you need to ask yourself if there's anyone else you are close to who is in need of medical or dental coverage. Can you claim a girlfriend to be your domestic partner? Are you able to get a friend or cousin added to your benefits list as a dependant? Is there someone you can creatively add to your benefits package in exchange for, say, free accommodation, meals or cash?

When you register someone to be covered under your benefits package, it's usual for your employer to check some information of that person in a database. Make sure that you list accurate information about the person you are claiming as a dependent, as if they don't show up in the database you will have some explaining to do. If you can argue that your dependent was born overseas, so they don't have a SSN, this may be a loophole you can exploit. If you adopt or foster a child, the benefits company only needs the adoption documentation, so you should be able to claim a child as a dependent with fake adoption or foster papers. You shouldn't need to submit a SSN: someone only needs a SSN if they are applying to pay into the social security system.

Sometimes employers will carry out audits to make sure that those you are claiming as dependents really are eligible. If you have chosen to add dependents who are really not eligible, this is where you may need to creatively use PDF-editing software to fabricate the documents they are looking for. Deciding not to supply the requested information is a bad idea. Give them what they are asking for and make it look credible. The risk here is that if you are discovered providing fraudulent information, you could be asked to pay back any benefit money you have received. You could also potentially be terminated from your employment and be prosecuted for fraud. This requires careful planning and consideration, depending on your circumstances.

You will see me refer to PDF-editing software several times. It is one of the few tools you will need to buy to profit from the concepts I'm describing in this book. PDF means "portable document format" and is an electronic format for saving documents which contain images and texts. There are many software types which can read a PDF & make it visible on your monitor or allow you to print it. However it takes special software to allow you to edit a PDF document. PDF-editing software is very powerful and useful for committing all kinds of fraud. If you want to edit a receipt or an invoice, you scan it, save it and then run an OCR (optical character recognition) utility that is built into the software. There are some free versions of these editing softwares, but I have not found any of them to be versatile enough. When I first started trying to manipulate documents I used some free software that converted the PDF to Microsoft Word, I edited in Word, then converted back to PDF. This was very cumbersome and usually gave major formatting issues where information was in the wrong place on the page or it just looked terrible for multiple reasons. Good PDF-editing software shouldn't give you these issues. OCR is especially powerful as it allows you to edit characters that might be recognized as pictures. You can convert these into text and in most cases have convincing looking documents. Expect to pay around $100 for some good software. Visit review websites to see which software is right for you.

EMBEZZLING EXPENSES

If you are fortunate enough to be able to buy items or to travel for your employer this is another great opportunity to line your pockets. Some companies will give you a credit card where they are billed directly for purchases you make. In some cases you will need to buy the items or pay for travel with your own credit/debit card, then file an expense report to get your money back. If you're given the choice it's often preferable to have someone else carry the debt, rather than yourself. However, sometimes there are more opportunities for expense embezzling if you pay for the items or the travel yourself, then file to get reimbursed.

Make sure you understand the company's rules and policies before filing expense reports. Some companies have limits on hotel and travel costs depending on the city you stay in. All companies have budgets and are aware of how much was spent in the previous year on a specific set of items or by a department. Companies usually have a minimum expense amount, maybe $20 or $50, above which you need to submit a receipt to get reimbursed. They also have a deadline each month when expenses need to be submitted. Make sure you submit expenses every month, so that managers and the finance department get used to seeing your expenses. If the deadline to submit your expenses is, say, the last Friday of each month, make sure you submit them on that day. Your manager will be rushed to approve them by her deadline and is much less likely to scrutinize them. Your goal is to extract as much money as possible from the company without breaking them, without raising any red flags, staying within the rules and guidelines as much as possible.

Let's say you have to go on a business trip to a convention. You need to get to the airport, get on a plane, stay at a hotel, eat some meals, go to some meetings then come home after a couple of days. You could take a taxi to the airport, or you could drive yourself, then pay to park there or you could just have a friend drop you off. Depending on the parking cost and the company's expense policy on receipts, the most lucrative deal for you might be to have a friend drop you off, but claim that you drove there and claim the parking expense. Understand how many miles it is from your house to the airport and pad this by whatever you think will reasonably be accepted. Whenever you have to travel for business it should never cost you any money personally. Whenever you are paying for any meal or service that your employer will pay for, make sure you tip very generously.

If you have to pay for your own expenses and then get reimbursed, there are some creative tricks that can be used. For airfares, you could have the airline email you a copy of the receipt and use PDF-editing software to change the amounts. If an airfare is booked several weeks in advance it will be less expensive. Figure out what it would cost booked a few days before you travel and claim this amount. This can also be done with hotels: stay at a reasonably priced place, but claim for a larger amount by editing the receipt, within the company's guidelines, of course.

I find meals are much easier to cheat with. Most companies will pay traveling employees for 3 meals per day, so make sure you claim for these. If they will pay, say, $30 without needing a receipt, submit each expense just under this without receipts. If someone else buys a meal for you, make a claim for that meal anyway, unless it's your manager.

If you need to rent a car while traveling, this is your chance to try a vehicle you would not normally drive. Again, understand what the limit is and stay within it; but only just. If you need to take a taxi, ask for a receipt. If you're paying with cash the taxi driver usually gives you a blank receipt. I prefer to fill these out as soon as I get out of the cab so I don't forget. Make sure you tip generously and write down a reasonably big number on the receipt. Embezzling taxi fares is easier than embezzling Uber rides: Uber payments are made electronically through credit cards, so are more traceable than cash payments made to taxis. However, if you are claiming expenses that you have paid yourself you can use PDF-editing software to change credit card statements.

Remember the importance of plausible deniability when embezzling; have responses planned out to issues that might come up. Here's an example of a scenario:

Salesman Joe is called into his manager's office after submitting his expense report.

Boss: "I see you made a charge on the company credit card at the Lonesome Cowboy Gentleman's Club. Can you explain this?"

Bad Response from Joe: "That wasn't me. I didn't make that charge."

Another bad response from Joe: "I lost my credit card so someone else must have done that."

Better response from Joe: "I had made arrangements to meet customer X there. I waited around but he didn't show up".

Even better response from Joe: "I met with the manager there and it looks like they are going to be a big new customer for our products. I'll have to go back there again next week to try to close the deal."

Some companies issue purchase cards (or P-cards) to employees who need to purchase large amounts of goods. Here again is another opportunity for some creative billing. Buy items for yourself, then figure out a way of reselling them. Need to order three new laptops for staff? Why not order four? Have items shipped to a vacationing coworker at another facility, but don't tell anyone. Intercept the item from the vacationer and resell it. These are just a few approaches that can be taken when you have access to company funds. You will get creative and depending on your circumstances you will come up with many more.

MAKING FREE PHONE CALLS

Companies often use conference call services so that their employees can connect with coworkers, suppliers and customers all over the world. They pay for a service, are given a phone number and purchase code numbers that come with leader personal identification numbers (PINs). Let's say a manager wants to set up weekly calls with his team members who are in numerous places around the world. He gives them the phone number and the conference code number to use to call in. The call can only start once the manager has entered his leader PIN, then everyone is connected. The company pays by the minute to the company that hosts the conference calls. Getting hold of this phone information is usually easy if you work in an office environment. Managers frequently pin this call information to their office wall. Sometimes they email it out to their employees so they can make calls without the manager's presence. Companies rarely check the usage history of these calls and managers are usually not even exposed to the billing process.

Once you have a manager's code number and PIN there are several things you can do with it. Share it with your friends so they can make free conference calls; this is especially useful for saving money on international calls, as domestic calls are almost free now, thanks to cell phones. You could sell the calling information to one of the company's competitors, who could call in when there are management calls happening. Senior management meetings are especially appealing in this case. Or you could have some fun and post the information online. Phone numbers that are used to call in to the service are obviously tracked so give this some thought before calling using your own personal phone.

Some years ago I obtained access to an executive secretary's online calendar. She had all of the executive's meetings on there and I gained access to his conference call information. I recall going out to a payphone and sitting in my car listening to one of their senior executive meetings. They discussed corporate strategy as well as completely inane topics. It was a real eye-opener.

Some companies offer cell phones to certain employees. They do this so they have the employee on a leash and can contact them. I like to refer to company-owned cell phones as tracking devices. The global positioning system (GPS) that's built into phones can be used to track your whereabouts. It's not a good idea to sneak out of work in the middle of the day and go to a bar with your phone on, just in case your manager decides to track your whereabouts. Turn it off in situations like this, leave it in the office or buy a faraday bag for it.

If your employer offers these phones, try to lobby your manager for one. The downside is that the company will often expect you to respond to calls and emails while you are on vacation. On the upside, you'll be able to make free personal calls, including international calls. You may be able to ditch your personal cell phone and just use the one your employer gives you. Alternatively you can carry two phones around with you wherever you go. You should be able to cancel your home internet service and use the company sponsored phone as a hotspot. When I was given a company cell phone I made sure to turn it off as soon as I left the office, unless I needed it for personal use.

Death Benefits

Insurance fraud has been taking place for as long as insurance companies have existed. The people at the insurance companies who investigate claims to make sure you are eligible are called Claims Adjusters and they are aware of every trick you could consider. When you make a claim it's in the company's interest to deny it as this will boost their profitability. One of the most complex insurance scams you can perpetrate is to fake your death so that your beneficiaries can claim on your life insurance policy. This is very difficult to do successfully in the USA, but slightly easier if you can arrange to fake your death and have a death certificate issued in another country. There are stories online of people who have obtained death kits from the Philippines, including death certificates. It could also be done in other developing countries. If you decide to go overseas to get a fake death certificate, research will be challenging and it's not something you can repeat if it goes badly. A better approach might be to have your partner-in-crime beneficiary submit a fake death certificate, fabricated with PDF-editing software. Doing this with official government documents is not easy due to the watermarks they often use, but can be done.

It's been said that faking your death by drowning is a bad idea. Insurance companies know that drowned bodies always wash up on a shore somewhere. Disappearing while hiking may be more readily accepted. It's also a good idea not to have your funeral staged as these can sometimes go awry.

Some employers offer life insurance policies at no charge, where beneficiaries would receive up to 100% of the employee's salary, or more by paying a small annual premium. The firms that administer this service for corporations are usually the same ones that administer other benefits. Just like any insurance company, they will have their own claims adjuster who will investigate the details of the death to make sure it's real. They will need a death certificate of the deceased person, which can usually only be given out once the identity of the dead body has been confirmed.

The authorities are more likely to issue a death certificate with no bodily evidence in situations where the person was exposed to "immediate peril". The State of New York issued death certificates for many people whose bodies could not be identified or found after the infamous September 11th 2001 attacks. This is also done for anyone thought to have been killed in battle. If there is no body or other proof of death, common law in most countries is to allow a death certificate to be issued seven years after the person is reported missing. If you claim on a life insurance policy and the person is later found alive you can expect to be sued, as well as to have to pay that money back.

One of the bigger challenges with faking your death is giving up everything you care about in your existing life. The older we get, the more attached we become to certain material items, even like certain items of clothing, jewelry and vehicles. It is also extremely difficult to give up on your loved ones, especially any children you may have, unless they are in on the fake death scheme. If they are conspirators, can you trust them? Another challenge is choosing the identity to use after your fake death. Once dead, your identity, SSN, credit and passport are essentially wiped clean. Do you have another ID that you can live under, possibly one you have legitimately borrowed from your friend or family member who has agreed to share it with you?

Kickbacks and Payoffs

Depending on your role in the company, you may be eligible to receive payoffs from suppliers or customers. Let's say you are a manager of a shipping department at a manufacturing company. Freight companies will offer to take you to lunch and bring you gifts in the hope that you will keep sending business their way. This is normal and is how business is done in most western societies. Some of these gifts can be trivial, like pens or doughnuts, but if you forge a good relationship with a supplier, you can make them an offer. Make it clear that you, and only you, are responsible for deciding which freight companies are used. Explain that right now you use 4 freight companies, but if the supplier is willing to pay you personally, off the books, that you will drop one of the other firms and send that business to them. Explain also that your employer treats you OK, but doesn't pay you what you need to support your lifestyle with five children, a sick wife and a dying mother. Make it clear that you are an otherwise decent person, looking for ways to bring in additional income. Gain the sympathy of the supplier. I have seen this approach work, but it comes with the obvious challenges. What happens when you go on vacation and someone else has to do the job and asks questions about your modus operandi? How long can you keep up this deceit? Do you find operating these schemes to be a thrilling challenge or do they keep you up at night? Anything that pulls so heavily on your conscience that makes you sick is probably not worth pursuing. But approaching something like this with the enthusiasm of an entrepreneur can give you a huge rush and be rewarding both financially and emotionally.

The healthcare system is especially rife with stories of kickbacks due to the huge amounts of money at stake in that industry. Doctors have been known to take payments from drug manufacturers to promote their products. In some cases doctors have made millions of dollars by prescribing questionable medications so they could be paid off by the drug companies. Some of these kickbacks have been monetary, disguised as speaking fees or payments for attending advisory meetings; some have been expensive trips, televisions and other consumer goods. In some cases doctors have accepted money for referring clients to specific hospitals, clinics and other health care facilities. When your doctor prescribes a medication or refers you somewhere, you need to make sure you are a well-informed patient and look out for your own best interests. Do not think that just because your doctor is politely spoken, clean-cut and well educated that he is above taking payoffs from deep-pocketed corporations.

Stealing Time

Your time is the most valuable thing you have. Once it's lost it will never return. There are a lot of conscientious folk out there who work excessive hours and want everyone to see that they work hard. That is not your objective. Your goal is to get the job done but most importantly it is to take care of yourself first, just as the corporation is taking care of itself first. If you are an hourly-paid (non-exempt) employee, you could have someone else clock-in or out for you every now and again. You could help them out in the same way. When the cat's away the mice will play, so take full advantage of your freedom when your boss is out of the office. Can you leave early for an appointment without disrupting the work of others too much? Can you develop a health problem that requires regular doctor visits? Get creative based on the situation you find yourself in.

Employers usually allow employees to take time off for occasional sickness. Make sure you use up all sick days you are given. When calling in sick it's best to call within a few minutes of waking up; this is when your voice will be most raspy and you will sound at your worst. Even though most companies don't have a definition of sick for the purpose of taking these days off, you don't want your boss to think you are just taking a day off to go to the amusement park with your friends. When I call in I never describe the problem. I will tell my manager that I need to take a sick day, or state that I'm feeling under the weather so sorry, I can't some in. If my boss asks about my problem I give a generalized response, indicating I would prefer not to discuss the personal nature of my health. A number of companies do not allow non-exempt employees to take sick days immediately after a public holiday or after already scheduled paid time off, so be careful how you handle this situation.

I was once an unhappy employee looking to find another job somewhere else. I'd been there a few years and had a good reputation for doing quality work. Once I started my job search I started explaining to my manager that I was having some major personal issues at home and that I wouldn't be able to travel overnight in the foreseeable future. Once I had identified a position that looked promising I stressed to him again that I was having some deeply personal issues and that I might need to take some time off in the future. I'm known by everyone as someone who keeps himself to himself, so he didn't pry or ask what my issues were. If he had asked me, I would have politely told him that I couldn't discuss the details. After a while I was offered the new job, so I told my existing boss that my personal problems had escalated and would it be OK if I worked from home for a while? I explained how things would work out & what I would do. He was sympathetic and immediately agreed. I started my new job while I was still on the payroll at my former company. This worked out well for a number of reasons. My new employer didn't offer medical benefits until I'd been there for 30 days. My old company was due to pay me a decent bonus that I wanted to get. If you know anything about bonuses you know that you have to be on the payroll on the day the payments are made or you don't get them. I also wanted to have as much income as possible. After a couple of weeks I started to get phone calls from my old boss, asking for me to call him. I had told my family that if anyone called asking for me they were to say: "He's not here right now; can I take a message?" I ignored all the calls. Eventually my boss's boss started to call me. Then one day the bonus checks were cut and I was eligible for benefits at the place I had been working at for over a month. So I called my former manager and handed in 2 weeks notice. They were exciting times.

This kind of co-employment can be conducted many ways. A friend's husband was at a job he didn't like so he took a leave of absence and went to work somewhere else, where he was paid a big signing bonus. He worked there for a while, but realized he actually preferred his previous job. So he went back to it and kept the signing bonus. I have seen employees accept a job with another company for more money, then wave that offer in their manager's face, demand they match the higher salary and get it. A manager will only fall for this approach once with any given employee.

If you have a job where you don't need to physically be at an office all the time, say in sales or delivery, this is often a perfect opportunity to set up and run a business on the side, work a second (or third) job or to take other liberties, depending on your desires. This is something I have done several times and it can be very rewarding. There are many books on the subject of running a part-time business, but what's important is to do something you are passionate about. Let's say you trade antiques on eBay: is this something you can do at work, creating the illusion you are doing what your manager thinks he is paying you for? If you are in sales, can you work two sales jobs at once?

You run the risk of losing credibility if both sales jobs are in the same industry, calling on the same clients, but if managed well you could take two completely different sales jobs where each management expects you are working forty hours per week, but you work each job four to five hours per day and come out ahead.

One of the reasons that most employees feel like trapped slaves is that they think like consumers. They assume that working for The Man is all they are capable of. Breaking out of that thinking is critical to breaking away from corporate slavery. Think like a producer, someone who is making and selling things into society, rather than as just a consumer or a doer of other people's tasks. Think of the kind of corporate theft I have described in these pages as a first step towards that freedom.

Faking Disability

Make sure that you fully understand your employer's policy on short-term and long-term disability as this is something else that can be gamed. If you become temporarily disabled and unable to work, say in a car accident or due to some surgery or illness, many companies will pay you while you go through your recovery. They will usually expect you to use up any unused vacation time for that year first as paid time off. If you still need time off after this they will allow you to take a certain number of weeks off as short-term disability (STD). Usually, STD will pay you up to 60% of your base pay for up to 4 months. If you need time off after this, you may then be able to take time off under their long-term disability (LTD) policy, usually at a lower salary percentage than with short-term disability. LTD payments are usually up to 50% of your base salary, but you can sometimes buy some additional insurance to extend that slightly when you sign up for company benefits each year. Many companies often don't have the resources to administer disability, so will outsource it to another company, who will offer this service to multiple other firms. This third-party company will have their own expectations of you that they have negotiated with your employer, so make sure you know what these rules are too.

Companies realize that employees will sometimes fake or exaggerate their medical conditions, which is why they pay you less of your salary while you are on disability. They know you want to be making your full salary, not a percentage of it, so they have established this system. But supposing you are legitimately sick or need time off to take care of some things and are willing to work for less pay. Maybe you want to explore another employment opportunity. Maybe your side business is ramping up. Or maybe you want time off to write a book. Taking short-term disability can often be a convenient way to accomplish this, as long as you are fine with the reduced income.

Taking advantage of a company's disability allowances usually requires some social engineering to be carried out. First, if you know you have surgery coming up, I find it's best to tell people you work with. This allows for some sympathy to kick in: both managers and fellow employees will start expecting less output from you. This will also allow the boss to start reallocating work if needed, which will ease the stress on those who will have to pick up your slack when you are gone. Making people aware of your condition, assuming you have one, will make it easier to take extended time off if you choose to, as everyone will already know you're not doing so well anyway.

Lying to the boss and especially to your co-workers can be the most difficult part. When most of us hear that a co-worker is not doing well we want to express concern and see if we can help. To minimize any guilt, you are better off exaggerating a condition, rather than totally fabricating something. Most people, when they hear of a sick colleague, encourage them to take all the time off work that they need. Take full advantage of these sympathies by doing exactly that.

If you choose to totally fabricate disability to get time off, it will be easier if this is done suddenly and without any warning. If you decide you were in a fictitious car accident, make sure it's far away from home, making it difficult for coworkers to visit you. If you can arrange for your sudden accident or illness to happen in another country, that would be even better. Have surgery & recuperate in another state. Many people know that some hospitals such as Mayo Clinic or those in Houston provide top-notch care, so it should be no surprise to them to learn that you are many miles from home getting good care at one of these facilities. You may not actually be at these places, but creating the illusion that you are can work in your favor.

In order to substantiate your short or long-term disability, the company that your employer has engaged to manage this function for them will require some documentation. You will need to provide doctor's notes and sometimes dates of surgeries. Make sure you know what condition you are exaggerating, understand all its symptoms and, if necessary, take medications to exaggerate these. Alternatively, if you are taking medications, you may be able to come off them for a while to fake symptoms. When you visit the doctor to initiate a disability claim, make sure that you look at your worst. Don't bathe, wear old, ripped clothes, walk slowly and deliberately or get yourself a wheelchair. If you are male, don't shave. Don't take illegal drugs as these can be found in drug tests, but otherwise do whatever it takes to get your doctor to believe your story.

In some cases the doctor's office may be contacted directly for verification, so do your research and make sure that you cover all the angles. If the doctor's office doesn't need to be contacted, but you have to provide documentation yourself for a fake or exaggerated illness, you may need to adjust some documents using your friend the PDF-editing software, depending on what is being asked for and what you can offer. Usually while you are on STD your medical and other benefits continue as normal. Once you go onto LTD, however, these usually only last for a few months or so, after which you will need to pay the COBRA rate. COBRA, or Consolidated Omnibus Budget Reconciliation Act of 1985, is a law that mandates that employees can get health insurance coverage after they leave their employers. Unfortunately, the cost of this is the full amount of what the employer pays, which will be several times what you, the employee, pays.

Some companies have restrictions and exclusions that apply when making disability claims. For example, if your illness was pre-existing before joining the company, or if you had a self-inflicted injury, you may not get coverage. Make sure you read all the fine print before going down the road to claim disability money. In some cases you may be better off claiming social security benefits for a long term illness or disability. You can game this in a similar way, but the government will have different requirements and it can take a long time to get a claim verified. If your performance is suffering at work and you think you might be disciplined or possibly terminated, make sure you tell your employer about health or disability problems immediately. It is more difficult to be terminated if you have a documented disability than if you are just seen to be incompetent.

Intellectual Property

One of the most valuable things a company has is not necessarily its facilities or equipment, but its intellectual property, or IP. This includes things like customer lists, expertise on making the company's products, patents, lists of employees and their capabilities, as well as knowledge of how the company provides services to customers.

If you are exposed to a company's IP it is worth collecting it, wherever possible. If you stay in that employer's industry it can be very valuable in the future, even if it is not up to date. Let's suppose you are in the finance department and encounter sales, customer and profitability information. That would be useful for you to have if you went to work for a customer, supplier or competitor. Many companies don't want to overtly buy stolen IP and this is not something that you can openly advertise as your reputation could be severely tarnished. However, if handled creatively, this information can be sold by setting yourself up as a consultant, ideally with an alternate name.

Creating an alternate name for business purposes is easy. If your name is John Smith you can open up a business account at a bank in the name of, say, Eric Williams. To open up the account you'll need to provide your real SSN, date of birth and address, but as far as the client is concerned you are Eric Williams. This reminds me of my favorite joke. A man placed an announcement in a newspaper: Mr. Norman Penis wants to inform everyone that he is changing his name; effective immediately, he will be known to everyone as Norm Penis. I digress.

IP can also be invaluable if you set up a company to compete with your employer. If you think this might be something you'd like to do, it's best to start slowly taking information a piece at a time as you come across it and cataloging it in a secure place. Trying to gather all the information you need in a day or so can prove to be very difficult and risky. Keep track of what you need and what you have actually taken. Stealing IP can be no more difficult than stealing office supplies if done correctly. In many cases it can be transferred onto a portable USB drive. When you get home, transfer it onto a computer. Companies keep logs of every electronic event that takes place, including the movement of information to portable drives. Unless you are working for the government they rarely do anything about it.

Suing Your Employer

There are numerous ways for an employer to get rid of an employee and in some cases you can take legal action against them to claim damages if this happens to you. Sometimes there's a downturn in the company's fortunes and they look at their financial statements and decide to shave a certain dollar amount or dollar percentage off the expense line. Sometimes a manager just doesn't like an employee so he decides she has to go. On occasions an employee is let go after being discriminated against: maybe the boss thinks that the employee is too old to handle things or that a black woman can't do the job. If you are suddenly summoned into an unexpected meeting with your manager and a human resources (HR) representative you need to cautiously assume the worst: that you are about to be terminated. In some cases your boss's manager will also be involved and sometimes it will be just HR. I have come across situations where employees have been let go en masse: called into a room and all told to be out by a certain time. I have heard of a case where a large team was called into a meeting and told that some of them would be let go. They were to go back to their workstations and wait for a possible phone call. If they were to stay with the company they would not be called. There have been many situations where a large group is offered early retirement: they get to go home early and be paid a pension or a severance package in exchange for signing a document and not coming back.

    The first thing to realize with any of these situations is that they are usually negotiable. So many times employees are offered a severance package and think it sounds great, so they sign the document that is put in front of them. It's in writing on company letterhead, so it must be official, right? Do not sign anything until you have had time to think about it. In the case of redundancies in force (RIFs) where the company feels they need to let go of a large number of the work force or they will go under, they will just pull you into an office individually, explain the situation, ask you to sign the document and lead you to believe that this is a good deal. They want you to accept it and will tell you that others have also been asked to leave under similar circumstances. Your best bet in this situation is to belong to a certain class of people: being a young white male does not put you in a strong situation if you want to start any legal action against the company. It's best if you are seen as a minority.

After being presented with the severance package and the document to sign, your best bet is to make sure you fully understand what you have been told, pick up the document, say nothing and walk out. This will give you time to think about the specifics of your situation. You have to decide if you want to stay employed there – possibly not – or if you would like to take legal action. In order to take legal action your first step is to contact the Equal Employment Opportunity Commission (EEOC), visit their website, eeoc.gov or to contact an employment attorney. The EEOC is a federal agency that administers and enforces workplace discrimination. You can take legal action against your employer if you feel you have any argument whatsoever that you have been discriminated against based on race, skin color, religion, sex (including pregnancy, gender identity and sexual orientation), national origin, age, disability or genetic information. Be aware that employment regulations vary from state to state. If you decide to fabricate or exaggerate some discrimination to strengthen your case, be aware that the person you are claiming discriminated against you will undergo questioning and possibly disciplinary action, maybe including termination.

The EEOC website is excellent and has all kinds of useful information that you should be aware of before you get called into that unexpected meeting. It's required reading for anyone working for an American company. There is an especially good section on Prohibited Employment Policies/Practices which describes how employers are not allowed to discriminate, including during the job advertising, recruitment, employment or termination processes. We've all heard about sexual harassment, but harassment for any reason relating to the above factors can give you a strong legal case to sue. Sometimes the act of starting legal action either through the EEOC or with an attorney can result in you and the company reaching a settlement, with you being better off.

DO NOT BREAK THE COMPANY

When taking from employers, do your best to be reasonable about it. Don't destroy the company in doing so. Don't be wasteful, taking things that you'll just throw out.

Not too many years ago, the vice president of finance at Koss Corporation, an electronics company, creatively embezzled $34 million over a period of several years and is still in federal prison as of this writing. She used the money to pay for her lavish lifestyle of clothes and vehicles. As a result employees suffered, pay was cut and some employees were laid off. The full story can be read online. I am not condoning this level of fraud which can destroy a corporation or hurt employees. I believe in a lower level of activity, taking a much smaller percentage of the company's wealth. In the case of the Koss fraud, the $34 million was about one year's turnover for the company and represented nearly half of its pretax profits over the fraud period. One of the ways she was able to get away with her acts for so long was that even though she needed to have her boss's approval to pay invoices over $5,000, no approval was needed to issue cashier's checks or wire transfers: the main way in which the funds were taken. Understanding how she was able to exploit this loophole may give you other ideas as you look at your own personal situation in a company. She became totally consumed with the embezzling that she couldn't stop. When she was finally caught she was completely relieved. Make sure that whatever theft you conduct is under your control and that you can stop at any time.

THINK LONG TERM

While you are working at a company, don't restrict your thinking to what is available today. Be aware of what you might be able to extract from them in the future. Do they give extra benefits to employees who stay for, say, five years? Are stock options, pension rights or annuities available? How might you take advantage of a company even after you've departed for one reason or another?

Some years ago a friend of mine worked for a large corporation and when he quit he did what everyone should do: he made sure he got every penny he was entitled to, as well as a few extra. Some years after he'd left, he had an unexpected letter from them, telling him he was entitled to pension benefits. When he looked through the package it was obvious they had him confused with another person with the same first and last names. This was a big company so he saw how this could happen, as his name is somewhat common. The papers gave him a set of instructions as to which options to chose: lump sum or different annuity options and how to sign the forms, get them notarized and send them back to the pension benefits administrator. Now, he knew he was not entitled to the benefits they described, but what did he have to lose? He followed the instructions and mailed the documents back. A couple of weeks later the pension benefits administrator mailed him back all his papers with a cover letter regrettably informing him that they had him confused with someone else. So sorry, but he wasn't entitled to anything that he hadn't already received.

At this point many people would have given up and thrown the papers in the trash. Instead he called the company and asked to speak to the pension benefits manager (the administrator's boss). He politely explained that he had some pension papers to submit and could he please send them to her to process? No problem, she told him. He got her name and location within the company. He typed out a very nice formal cover letter addressed specifically to her, requesting that she please process the enclosed forms. He mailed everything to her specifically and not too long after this he received a nice check in the mail, which he promptly deposited into an IRA account.

Why did this work? Why was he able to get this money from them that he was not entitled to? He was betting on a number of things falling into place. First, he was betting these days, but if you work for such a place you might be able to figure out how to intercept pension payout information from them in other ways.

Planning for the future can also include getting information on the potential benefits that others may be entitled to. You don't want to deprive a fellow worker of any of these benefits, but if you can fraudulently make claims on their benefits, the employer will still be required to pay them, while you may have been able to intercept money and run off with the company's funds.

that the pension benefits administrator didn't tell her boss when she first mailed him someone else's paperwork. When you make a mistake at work do you tell your manager? You probably don't. If you're like most people, when you realize you've messed up you clean up the mess you made and keep quiet about it. If you tell your boss every time you make a mistake it won't be too long before they let you go. Think of it as covering up. This aspect of employment is something that can be taken advantage of in many ways. Catch an employee at a corporation making a mistake in your favor and there's a decent chance you'll get away with it. Employees care more about their own skins than about company assets. I know that I do.

Second, he was betting that the pension benefits manager was not good at delegating. I have seen this with some managers, who are so autocratic and pompous, that they feel they have to do everything themselves. If she were a good manager, she would have handed his paperwork to the administrator when she received it and it would have been denied right there. The administrator is supposed to handle and process the forms and submit them to her boss for approval. The manager then submits the payments for processing. His application skipped a layer of approvals.

Third, he was betting that the other ex-employee with the same name as him didn't submit his paperwork before my friend's was processed. Now, my friend knows this company and is sure that when the other guy submits his paperwork, they will pay him. I can just imagine the lively discussion in the office when his paperwork arrives with the administrator and is submitted for approval.

Several months later, when the manager realized that my friend had money he wasn't entitled to, she wrote him a stern letter, explaining the misunderstanding and demanding he pay them back with interest. That letter went straight through my friend's shredder. At this point he made the same assumption that he had made before: that she wouldn't be telling her manager about the missing money. It's one thing to send the wrong papers to someone, but to send money to the wrong person is very much frowned upon in companies. It seems he was right: a number of years later he hasn't heard from that company any more and has the statute of limitations working in his favor. It's just as well he has no plans to work there ever again. Many companies don't offer pensions

Becoming a Whistleblower

The government (state and federal) is also very keen to take advantage of corporations in some situations. In fact, they will grant protection to individuals who blow the whistle on corporate wrongdoing where the government is losing out, such as in cases of Securities and Exchanges (SEC) fraud or taxation issues. If you find your employer is breaking the law and, especially if you feel they are in some way taking advantage of the government, you can report this to an attorney and if the case is successful you can get up to 30% of the proceeds. In the last five years the US government has paid out over $107 million as rewards. A relatively recent payout was to a Monsanto executive who benefited to the tune of around $22 million after he blew the whistle on the company which was found guilty of SEC fraud and forced to pay over $80 million.

In another recent case, Genesis Healthcare Inc. was required to pay almost $54 million to reconcile claims that they provided medically unnecessary care and that the care they provided was substandard. In addition they allegedly billed the government for this. Seven whistleblowers received almost $10 million as a result of the company's violations of the False Claims Act. The company suffered and the whistleblowers gained.

There are several federal laws which provide protection to the blower and stipulate that rewards are paid. These include the False Claims Act, the Dodd-Frank Financial Reform Act, the Occupation Safety and Health Act (OSHA). Some states have their own laws that offer protection and rewards to employees who report fraud at the state level. The Internal Revenue, SEC and Commodity Futures Trading Commission (CFTC) also offer protection and rewards.

Blowing the whistle on corporate malfeasance is not easy. You need to hire an attorney, be prepared to be discovered (even though you will have protection from termination or demotions or other punishment). Just identifying the problem usually isn't enough. Whistleblowers usually have to work hard to provide significant evidence to the government and expend a lot of energy to keep the case going, all the while not being sure they will actually win out and gain financially at the end of the day. If you see wrongdoing at a corporation you need to decide if you want to tell an executive or blow the whistle through an attorney. This is not a do-it-yourself process and certainly needs professional legal help to navigate the minefield. There are law firms who specialize in cases like this and would be the best ones to start with, rather than approaching a generalist lawyer.

Exiting a Company

Everyone ends up leaving a company for one reason or another, whether it's voluntarily or involuntarily, for another job, to set up a company or to retire. If you leave voluntarily you will want to take as much of the company's property with you as you can, whether it's intellectual property, funds or just office supplies. The best time to gather up what you plan to take is before you announce your departure to anyone.

If you're planning to leave your employer I find it's best to avoid even hinting that you might be leaving. I like to openly tell my boss that I love working there and that I plan to be there forever. I once had a manager who told me I could totally trust her and that if I was ever planning to leave the company I should just go to her and discuss it. I wonder how many people fall for that. Once you tell your manager you're looking into leaving they immediately start planning to replace you in one form or another. Word spreads like wildfire throughout the organization that you're leaving. One person tells another in confidence, who then tells another, in confidence. It's not long before people you've never met come up to you in the corridor and tell you they are sorry to hear you're leaving, even when you haven't even secured another job. If you genuinely feel that you can negotiate a better deal by threatening to leave, think long and hard about that strategy. Your instincts will tell you the extent to which you can negotiate. Only announce to your manager that you are leaving once you know you have secured your future and that, if you are going to another job, that you have passed any pre-employment screening.

Once you quit, you can expect the unexpected. Employees often feel like they should do the decent thing and give two or more weeks' notice. If you have a unique skill, employers may ask you to work out your notice or try to get you to stay for longer while they find your replacement. For specialized positions it's often very difficult to find a replacement in two weeks. Sometimes employers will decide that you are leaving within minutes of you giving notice and that they will only pay you until the end of that day. You should assume this could happen, even though you feel like you're doing the right thing by giving a couple of weeks' notice.

It's always worth being aware of how other employees are treated when they quit. If they are treated badly, there's a good chance you will be too. For professional positions it's common to be escorted to your office to gather up your personal items when you quit, then escorted off the property. The manager then instructs human resources to pay you until the end of the pay period. This has happened to me twice. What this means is that you should be very aware of the pay cycles within a company and make sure you can maximize your income around them. Don't hand in your notice the day before a pay cycle ends unless you have a good reason.

Managers often feel like they need to give the impression they are in charge and in control. If other employees see the boss escorting you out of the building they assume that the boss has initiated the termination. That just reinforces the image that they are in charge. Managers usually don't want to give the impression that a subordinate is calling the employment shots. Once you've left, managers often tell your former coworkers that you are "no longer with the company" or that you "left to pursue other interests". They feel that this politically correct jargon gives the impression you were terminated by the boss, whether it's true or not.

Whichever way you look at your situation, if you are planning to leave, you need to take anything and everything that will be useful to you at least a day before you make the announcement. This includes any of your personal items, as it will probably be difficult to go back to get anything you forget.

SUMMARY

Working for corporations may suck, but there is a lot you can do to make your stay there tolerable. Develop a positive mental attitude towards life and focus on not being taken advantage of. There are a number of legitimate ways in which you can maximize your income from companies. As you spend more time there you will find some approaches which are not so legitimate, but are fine to practice anyway, given how corporations treat us.

My goal with this book is to get you to understand that you will not be totally fulfilled working for a corporation, but that there are many things you can do to ease the stress and discomfort that comes with the corporate existence. Make sure that you treat everyone with respect and dignity and give them plenty of assistance as they too make their journey through corporate life.

If you have any feedback or want to discuss any points privately please reach me through my website:

www.HowToScamCorporations.weebly.com.

Best Regards,
Lucas Anderssen

www.ingramcontent.com/pod-product-compliance
Lightning Source LLC
Chambersburg PA
CBHW031549210526
45464CB00003B/1223